Bending
BUT NOT
Breaking

TOHNYONAH JACKSON

To Liz,
Thanks for your
Support. God Bless!!

INTRODUCTION

Habakkuk 2:2-3 *Then the Lord replied: Write down the revelation and make it plain on the tablets so that a herald may run with it. For the revelation awaits an appointed time; it speaks of the end and will not prove false. Though it linger, wait for it; it will certainly come and will not delay.*

As I started to write this book, it was put on my heart and my spirit to tell how God works through tough times, even when you don't know much about him as a child or as an adult; he knows all about you. He knows how He's going to use you before you even know how to ask how to be used. He preps us from the beginning. Our preparations are our storms. As we go through our storms we must trust and know that he is right there with us. What don't break you will make you. Just know that the greater Blessings come with greater storms. Just know he will not send a storm your way without covering you and preparing you first.

There are places God wants to take you and when He's ready for you; don't be surprised that some of those you call BFF or the favorite family members in your life are not going to be able to go with you. Some of them you may outgrow, others may just walk away from and some you lose due to death. I lost my mother, my aunt (who was like a mom to me), and the loss that took everything from me was losing my grandmother. I lost a friendship of twenty plus years, all within fifteen months. I lost all that mattered to me, but when God is in the process of showing who He is, He has to remove all of you and replace it with all of Him. God has a way of taking everything from you so you can just depend on Him. It is his way of saying, "It has been me all this time. Now that I have you to myself, now I can do my business with you." So, as you read this book you will understand why these women meant so much to me in my life and the different places in my heart they hold.

As I allow you to travel through this journey of my life to show you how God used a baby, a teen, and a young adult to show His work of making a diamond in the rough. Reading this story, I want you not to focus so much on the sad and hurtful things, but to focus on how God will take you through the storm and cover you without your knowing according to His will. There were and still are many things that have affected me throughout my life. I have used my experiences to build on my foundation of trusting God and to strengthen my faith within Him. God can take nothing and make something.

As a child, I lived in two homes; trying to find out where I belonged; a family where verbal and physical abuse was the norm, a family where no one wanted to admit that anything was their fault but was ready to spread the blame, a family where hatred, selfishness and molestation had run rampant for two generations. A family where no one wanted to disrupt their comfortable lives by talking about the relationship between mothers, daughters and other family members, a family where no one wanted to put an end to the confusion and madness, a family that had everything and yet, had no heart, a family that used their money to cover the dysfunction.

God is still molding me for His purpose. I am not perfect at this point, but what I can say is that I'm SAVED. Hopefully, my story will glorify Him, inspire, and encourage others throughout this journey called life.

INDEX

Chapter 1   *My Vision or My Nightmare* *9*

Chapter 2   *The Start of Being Violated* *13*

Chapter 3   *The Love of another that's not your own* . *16*

Chapter 4   *Had about Enough* *20*

Chapter 5   *The Little Things That Mean So Much* . . . *23*

Chapter 6   *No Rules No Boundaries* *27*

Chapter 7   *A Baby having A Baby* *31*

Chapter 8   *Refused to be a Statistic* *36*

Chapter 9   *Another Let Down* *43*

Chapter 10 *Daddy's Home* *49*

Chapter 11 *It's Time to Go* *55*

Chapter 1

MY VISION OR MY NIGHTMARE

Genesis 1:1-2 *in the beginning God created the heavens and earth. Now the earth was formless and empty, darkness was over the surface of the deep, and the Spirit of God was hovering over the water*

I am feeling as if my head is held under water with the enemy holding me by the back of my neck. My hands are tied behind my back and the only breath I get is when God demands him to let go. God gave the enemy permission to do as he wanted, but he could not kill me because, as we know, he has no authority and he has to ask for permission to tamper in our lives (Job 1:6-12). As he's holding my head under water, I am visualizing my life. I can't breathe; no one is helping me because they can't hear me because I am crying for help with my head under water. When God says, "Let go", I get a chance to breathe. I'm trying to catch my breath so I can cry for help. I want to fight, but why should I? Everything that the enemy is telling me seems to be true.

When he raises me up to breathe, he pulls my head back and I hear whispers of him telling me, "Give up with the life you have, it's not worth living. You're bitter, angry, a loner, you can't finish high school, you will be another statistic, a teenage mother with nothing." Back under the water he puts my head. I'm visualizing again. My mom was addicted to drugs; I was molested at five by a man that was to be my grandfather, adopted by a family that clearly had no idea how to love a child that needed love and again sexually violated by family members of this family. My son father cheated on me and had another baby a few weeks after our son was born that I had no idea of. We planned together to have him and I just knew we was going to be a family but that changed within weeks.

This was the man I thought I would be with the rest of my life. I am bitter; I am mad, I don't know how to trust or even if I want to trust again. I stay to myself because I don't like to give anyone my problems. It's not anyone's business since all they are going to do is talk about me. Maybe the enemy is right, maybe I have no reason to fight for life; maybe I'm better off gone. "There is not a man alive that's going to want you as a wife, you have too much baggage. No one cares about you; if they did they would have been there for you from day one. You see how your family let you go and no one wanted to care for you as a child? Do you really think they care about you as an adult?"

Why am I being put through this? Why did I have to have a family filled with drugs and alcoholism; a family that did not allow me to have a mother's love, a family where alcohol and drugs broke the bond between a mother and her children? The fighting, due to the issues that this family is dealing with, and no one wants to admit to their own faults and wrongs so they blame each other. Hatred towards each other because they are allowing the enemy to take control and have his way. The selfishness of the ones who don't care about anyone but themselves and stay away because they don't want to be bothered. They have their own comfortable lives. A mother and daughter hating each other as if they were strangers, and molestation going on in the home through two generations, yet no one wants to bring it to an end due to the confusion of one's own life.

I was taken out of that home only to be put in a home where everyone wanted to be part of that family because on the outside, it looked like the Cosby Show and on the inside; it was living hell. Taken into a family where money spoke for everything and instead of dealing with the issues in the house, they covered it up. Swept under the rug so no one can see it. Send what is not the problem away, wash their hands and go on with life as if nothing happened.

Oh, how God's angels and Satan's angels are fighting for me while I'm under water. I hear God's angels saying, "God has a plan for you young lady, don't you give up. This battle is not yours, this battle is the Lords, these Goliaths in your life are not yours, they belong to your mother, father and grand-mother and because they didn't handle them; you have been chosen to handle it, fight, and stand. When you fight; God will give you the victory and he will get the glory." I will be a victor not a victom

"The voice of the enemy is a lie. He is here to kill your spirit, kill your trust, and have you to take your life. He is here to steal; to steal your joy, your love, your peace, and your heart. He is here to destroy; to destroy your family, your faith in God, and your mind because that's his job. He knows God has something great for you so you need to allow God to break the curse the enemy has on the lives of you and your children. Satan has no control. God only allows him to do so much with you; he does not have all power over your life. He does not have the final say."

Lord, where is the first link to this chain so I can break it? Lord Jesus, I need another good breath so I can break

11

this chain. The next time he lets me up out this water, I'm breaking these chains. I will not be tied to this madness anymore. He will not have a hold of me any longer. I will bend, but I will not break. These chains are broken.

Chapter 2

THE START OF BEING VIOLATED

LUKE 18:16 *Let the little children come to me, and do not hinder them, for the kingdom of God belongs to such as these. Truly I tell you, anyone who will not receive the kingdom of God like a little child will never enter it.*

As a 5-year-old sitting in a kindergarten class, you would think of an innocent baby enjoying playing with friends and blocks and learning ABC and numbers. But not me. I was feeling uncomfortable in areas of my body that was not supposed to be touched with pain and discomfort. As I remember, my teacher walked me to the office having had some concerns about my body behavior and wanted me to be checked out. After sitting there for a while, a lady came in and she began talking to me about why she was there. I don't remember exactly how the conversation went but I do remember telling her what was hurting and who was doing it.

Back in those days they used dolls to describe where, when and how you were being touched and what was being said so she pulled out this doll and asked, "Where did he touch you?" I pointed down between the dolls legs and said, "Right here." Then she asked, "What did he use?" "His fingers" I replied. She asked, "Can you show me how he did it?" I showed her. My grandmother's husband had molested me. He had this chair that sat by the window and he would make me sit on his lap and do the ungodly things with his hands. It would hurt which would cause me to say, "That hurt" but he would tell me to be quiet and not to tell anyone.

My mom was not there, my grandmother worked a lot and my aunt was there sometimes. This was a very dysfunctional home and nothing was much in order so whatever happened there was normal for me. God gives us the family he knows that is best for us. (Jeremiah 29:11-14) As I waited after the lady left, I was escorted out with the police and I had to ride to a place where I didn't know anyone. I thought I was going home but it seems there were other plans. Since this was not the first time I had been in the police car; I thought this was another one of those rides. This was the last ride. I was by myself with nobody but the strange people that were around me.

Before my final departure from my biological family, I lived with my grandmother's sister who would dress me up in cute dresses and take me to church. It was fancy with her all the time. I was really feeling like a princess with my Aunt and then back to my grandmother's house. I would stay with my other aunt; she had her own baby by then but before she had her baby I was her baby. She was always open to take me and treat me as if I was her own. She had been my mommy before she had her own daughter. My grandmother worked two jobs and would take me to work sometimes with her on her second job. If I told her I wanted something, she was going to make sure I got it. As I can remember, my grandmother always drove trucks and loved me with everything in her and I loved her too, and still do.

As I arrived to a big building and realized I wasn't going home, it started getting scary for me. Alone in a place and not knowing anyone for a five-year-old can be scary. I sat in this foster home looking out with my two big ponytails and a mouth full of silver caps in my mouth looking out for my grandma to come get me because I knew she was coming. She always came and got me. Well this time was different because she didn't come and if she did; I didn't see her. My mom came and I remember seeing her crying through the glass. I couldn't talk to her or see her and at that moment I was thinking, "Is anybody coming to get me, does anybody want me? Why am I here because I thought I was going home?" Just a lot running through this five-year-old mind. After a few days went by, everyone told me everything was going to be ok and I think that was just to take my mind off of what was really going on. I became numb to the fact that this was it. I believe this is when I started becoming numb to everything and having no kind of stability or care in my life.

Chapter 3

THE LOVE OF ANOTHER THAT'S NOT YOUR OWN

Isaiah 41:13 *for I am the Lord your God who takes hold of your right hand and says to you do not fear I will help you.*

I saw this light skinned, heavyset woman; she was smiling at me and looked real friendly. I was told that that was who I was going home with. As I arrived at this house, it was a big house with a park right across the street and all I could think about was playing at the park every day. As I got in the house, I was amazed at how big it was. So many rooms, a big backyard; just a house that you would dream of back in that day. She had three biological sons, but she had no birth girls. It looked like these people were rich.

I was a little shy, not scared though, I have already been with people I didn't know and at this point, I was just watching everyone and not saying much. There was another girl there but after a little while, she was gone and it was just me. At that point I was called, "Baby girl." I was the only girl for a little while. I enjoyed being a little girl there. Everyone was so nice to me and made me feel welcome and made me feel like I was part of a family. I felt like I was loved. There was a mommy and a daddy in the house; there were two dogs, a fence around the house, nice vehicles–not just one, but three. This was considered rich.

All the time I still missed my grandma. I'm still waiting for her to come get me because she always come. I didn't think that this move was permanent so I just went with the flow because I was able to continue to go the same school and still see my same friends so it wasn't too bad. Until I had to go to another school, close by the house. I didn't understand why because everyone else in the family was going to one place and again I was separated to go alone to another school. By me saying that the mommy was the counselor at my school and her son went to the same school, why did I have to be moved to go to another school? Although I didn't know anyone, I did meet friends from the neighborhood that I went to school with so that was a good thing because I had friends I could play with on the weekends. I later I went back to Millwood where everyone else went as a family.

It was a normal day at school then I got a message to come to the office because there was someone who wanted to see you. I got to the office, sat down, and who came through the door? It was my grandmother! My eyes were filled with completeness, happiness and joy. I was so happy but confused also, because I thought my grandmother had given up on me and didn't want to see me anymore. Now, I remind you that I was adopted by now and my adopted mother didn't have to allow me to see my grandmother at all (but when God has a plan, there is nothing no one can do to stop it). I was able to start going to visit my grandmother on weekends.

I loved when the weekends came because I was able to see my cousins and other family that I missed. I would spend the night on weekends with my grandma, she would cook greens, cornbread, a roast, okra, all kinds of food and I loved my grandma's cooking. Even now my cousins and I would laugh because I was the only one that thought my grandma could cook. When the weekend was over and I had to go home, my heart was so broken because I knew I was going back and didn't want to cause I loved my grandma so much I didn't want to be separated from her. I would cry and I remember her telling me, "Toot, stop crying 'cause if you cry, she's not going to let you come back. So wipe your face before she gets here." I would clean my face and she would tell me, "I will see you next weekend ok?"

After a while my Aunt Nee Nee would come get me and I would spend some weekends with her too. She would pick me up on Fridays and we would go to El Chico's and eat and bring back chips and salsa, and watch wrestling on TV. Sometimes we would even go to the wrestling matches when they would come to town. It was as if I was released from prison every weekend from this house that was to be home. The one thing about my visits was that I was able to visit everyone but I was not allowed to see my mom. My grandma wanted me to see my mom but if she did then I wasn't going to be able to visit grandma again. That kept a lot of confusion still going in my family.

Well, while I was visiting my grandma, my mom got wind of it and started coming around but I wasn't allowed the time with my mother as I was with my grandmother and aunt due to my mom's addiction. That was what I was told but I really feel there was more to it, but I did see her and I didn't feel comfortable with her because I had never spent time with her before I was taken. To be in her presence wasn't the same as it was with my grandma and aunt. It seems like there was always an argument with her and my grandma because I wasn't supposed to be around her and if my adopted mom would come and see her there, my grandma would lose her privileges with me so my mom would have to leave and it was always a big deal.

After a while, there was another girl in the family who looked more so like she belonged in the family. She was older than me and had a lot more going on than I did. She would always get in trouble and catch all kind of hell and I didn't understand why she was always getting whippings and having to do so much around the house. I would watch how she would have to cook, clean and take a lot of heat from the people in the house and I didn't understand until later. Soon she left and didn't come back, but she did stay in touch. After she left then I had took her place. Cooking, cleaning, washing, ironing; like a little maid.

I got to enjoy being a kid up until about the time I was nine or ten, when the beatings became more frequent and then the son started coming into my room at night with the ungodly activities. Every night, I would hate to fall asleep because just as I would fall asleep, I would hear the rubbing of the bottom of the door going across the carpet of my bedroom floor. The door would rub on the carpet because it was nice and blush, I would clench up and just lay there and hope he would change his mind and leave out, but he didn't. He would come in my room, get in my bed, and just do what he wanted to do. He would try to force things on me that just made me feel like a dirty rag. I would move my face, but I still tried to act like I was asleep, then after he finished doing what he wanted with me, he would leave a mess behind for me to clean up myself.

I was so hurt and disgusted with my life at this point because there was no one for me to talk to. There was nothing that this boy did that was wrong in his mother's eyes. If I would've told what was going on, who would've believed me? So I took the abuse and dealt with it. This woman had so much power to where no one would cross her about anything and she knew everybody. It was the things I was dealing with that on the outside, you would had thought this family had it all together but in reality it was a lot of abuse mentally and physically going on. I wouldn't say anything because of the position she had.

Chapter 4

HAD ABOUT ENOUGH

James 1:12 *Blessed is the one who perseveres under trial because, having stood the test, that person will receive the crown of life that the Lord has promised to those who love him.*

At around twelve years old, I was sick of that house and my mind was on self-destruction mode; not caring about anybody. I was on edge. I didn't care anymore, whatever happened to me happened, I wanted to end my life and others too.. My life as I saw it was like a nightmare with my eyes open. I was tired of the beatings, the verbal abuse, the put downs and not having anyone to talk to. Where was the God that my aunt and my mom told me about? Where was the man who made me? You could not tell me that Jesus loved the little children because if he did; why is he allowing all this? I wasn't a bad kid but I wasn't a good kid either. I was just a little girl with some issues.

There was no one for me to go to in the time of need. I called the other girl that was there in the home that had experienced the same abuse and told her I didn't want to be there anymore, so she came to get me. When I got off the phone with her I walked to the corner of the long dirt and rocky driveway and they were waiting for me. I got in the car and was gone for a few weeks. It wasn't the best that I wanted but to be away from that house at night, I felt like I was in heaven. I walked the streets with no extra clothes and no food, thinking, "What do I do now? Where is God? I'm lost and can't find my way but I'm not going back to that house." At this point, I was thinking, "I will live in the street before going back to that house. She can send me where ever she wants but not to that house."

I would go to my friend's house to stay a little while and then leave. KNOCKING. Every time I heard a knock at the door my heart would hit the floor. This time there was a knock and I heard a voice that said, "Is Tohnyonah over here?" When I heard that voice, I felt like I could run straight through her and run until I couldn't run anymore. I came out of the room because I didn't want any problems with my friend and her mom. I got in the car and my adopted mom took me to St. Anthony's 2 North (Psych Ward). When I got there, I didn't care at this point I was numb to everything. I was thinking, "So I'm crazy now?"

Being in that place was an experience. There were people there with way more issues than I had, but the funny thing was; I would have rather been there with them than in the house of destruction. When I arrived, the windows were thick like bulletproof glass and you couldn't raise them up. I could write and had limited phone calls so I would talk to my best friend. I would go home on the weekends but I didn't want to go, I had rather stayed in the hospital than to be there. I was still in the mind frame of not going back when I got out. So when it was time for me to get ready to go home I told them that if I go back I'm leaving again, and I left again. By this time, she was tired of me and I was tired of her and that house so when she got me from my best friend's house and back to the hospital I went. I was there for a few days and then straight to the bus station from there. Her words to me as we were headed to the bus station were, "Before I let you ruin my family's name, I will send you away."

OK, I see God making some moves now but he was making them from the beginning; I just didn't know. I was so happy and didn't care where I was going as long as I was away from that house. I was happy, so when she told me she was sending me to Iowa with my aunt my heart was racing at 5000. I was so happy and couldn't wait to see her. I missed her so much. It was a long ride but I didn't have anything but time. I had time to think about this God I was always hearing about and why all this was going on. Why so much heartbreak for a kid like me? God where are you? What took you so long to get me away from the madness?

When I got there, my cousin was there to pick me up from the bus station. I was so happy to see my cousins and my aunt. When I got to her place, it was a studio apartment and it was her and her two kids living there. She opened up her door for me with what she had. She didn't have a lot of money nor did she make any groan about me being there. Even though it was a small space, that was the best time I had in my life. I enjoyed being in that little space with people I loved and I knew loved me, more than being in a big space where I felt like killing myself. I'm not going to lie; I gave my aunt a few run arounds but I was being a thirteen/fourteen-year-old girl. One thing she never did was give up on me and I love her so much for it.

Chapter 5

THE LITTLE THINGS THAT MEAN SO MUCH

LUKE 16:10 "*Whoever Can Be Trusted With Very Little Can Also Be Trusted With Much And Whoever Is Dishonest With Very Little Will Also Be Dishonest With Much*

My first day of school and I know no one, not a soul. I was the new girl and I had the new girl blues. I did end up with two friends. I was lucky to have a boyfriend (He was a boy who became my best friend. We still talk today.) His name was Clyde. He helped me find the bus stop, helped me around school; he was just one of the greatest people at our age there was. He was like the big brother I never had. Today, I can still call him and he gives me what I need to hear, not what I want to hear. God places people in our lives for seasons and it just so happen that our season of friendship is still growing.

There was a girl name Kesiah that I became friends with too. I loved the relationship she had with her family. They didn't have a lot but they had love for each other and that was what counted. She was my friend at school also. We would go to the mall together and I would go over her house, but when I had to go to another school, our friendship kind of faded. Nothing bad, I just think the move to another school and meeting new friends changed our friendship. We had become really good friends but after I left JB I didn't talk to her anymore.

I ended up with more guy friends than girls. The boys were more down to earth to be around; I found that the boys were friendlier than the girls were because the girls didn't like me and never got to know me. I was always getting into issues with people at school, So I had to go to different schools. I went to three schools in just my freshman year of high school. No stability through my freshman year in high school. I guess I was warming up to the new town, I guess. The last school I went to I met another close friend. I met her at Smart Jr. High. She wore a Green Bay Packer jacket and she had braces. We started hanging out and let's say we did not need to be together we were always doing something. We would meet at school and we would leave school and go to Rock Island and be back before school was out. She was the first person that introduced me to "Across the bridge." Across the bridge was what divided Ill and Iowa apart which made it the Quad City area. We would have so much fun together. We talked about everything and were there for each other. We were always together; she was like my sister, my next best friend because Kenisha was my best friend so it took me a while to meet someone because no one could take her place.

After being in Iowa for a while, not much of the year, my mom moved there with my two little brothers. I missed them so much; they would just cling to me when I saw them, especially my baby brother. I was staying with my aunt and my mom would come around but I never really clung to her because I didn't know her like that and I was at that adolescent part of my life where nobody could really tell me anything so I really didn't want her speaking to me. In my mind, I'm wondering, "Where you been? What have you been doing? What were you doing when my life was a living hell. Now that I'm thirteen you want to come in my life; I'm really not feeling you lady."

It was report card time and my grades were trash. I think I had some D's, F's, and maybe a C. Not good at all and my aunt was so mad at me, I really disappointed her. She called my mom over and that was the wrong thing to do but I don't think my aunt knew it would get physical. My mom came over with an attitude and started comparing me to my brothers. I wasn't really listening to anything she was saying because I didn't care what she was saying, so when she went to grab me the fight broke between her and me in the studio apartment. So much anger and rage was in me and I took a lot of it out on her. To me, she was a stranger. She didn't know how I was feeling on the inside but she was also hurting on the inside too from her own issues.

Then my other aunt came over and she started in on me, so now I have my family turning on me, fighting me, and I'm a child with ticking time bomb issues going on. My thought was, "Why are these strange people putting their hands on me? I don't know them and I haven't done anything for them to come in and start putting their hands on me. A few days go by and there was a knock on the door. It was a man and a woman. I didn't answer the door, but by that time my aunt was coming home she met them at the door and they wanted me. Apparently someone called them to tell them that I was a danger to myself and others. I wasn't talking to them or hearing anything they had to say because I was still upset about what was going on from the past few days. As I sat there, ignoring what they had to say, they asked me was I willing to go with them or were they going to have to force me to go? I wasn't going willingly so they had to force me. I didn't feel like I did anything wrong so why should I go with these people and I was not an easy go. I couldn't understand why I was being bothered so much I just wanted to be left alone. I was tired of looking at white people and the only time I come in contact with them is when they are taking me somewhere." So much was going through my mind and at that point I was ready to fight back. I'm wasn't going anywhere, was tired of white people taking me somewhere, I never came across one to try to help me.

I ended up in another Psych hospital. Again, they were trying to give me some meds that I knew I didn't need and wasn't taking. I had two of my friends coming to see me; Clyde and my other good friend from Smart. They would catch the bus to see me and I knew that they were my real friends. After a few weeks went by, there was a hearing. Both my aunts, my mother and I were there. I was so mad I didn't want to talk to nobody but my Aunt Nee Nee. Well, it came out to where I could leave and didn't have to stay in that place another day. I didn't want to have anything to say to them.

Going back home with my aunt, so many things were going through my mind. I was becoming numb to the fact that this was going to be my life. Either in and out some mental hospital when there is nothing wrong with me and everyone is trying to make something wrong with me, or I was going to be in and out of jail because it seems like the only peace I got was when I was locked down. As I look back on it all it seems to me the enemy wanted me to go crazy and lose my mind so I wouldn't be able to give God the praise that I do today. But again, he can only do what God allows him to and when you're chosen, you're covered.

Chapter 6

NO RULES NO BOUNDERIES

Colossians 3:20 *Children, obey your parents in everything, for this pleases the Lord.*

After making amends with my mom from not speaking to her for a long time; I started feeling as if I wanted to spend more time with her and wanted a relationship with her. Here is where I see now God moving and working. Mending the relationship that I wanted so bad now coming together. As my Aunt prepared to move to California with my grandma I was confused on if I wanted to stay with my mom or go with my Aunt. It was such a hard decision to make for myself. Did I want to stay with my mom? Yes, I did. Did I want to go with my Aunt? Yes, I did. But I decided I wanted to live with my mom and my brothers. I missed my aunt when she left, but I was glad I was with my mom and brothers. But it wasn't all good as I thought it would be. There were really no rules for me at fourteen. I got to do whatever I wanted to do. I was having boyfriends older than me with cars and my mom never questioned me about who, what, when, where, how, or why. She was living her own life. I'm not saying that she didn't love her kids, but the addiction had her gone.

When my mom wasn't high, she was the best person you could meet. She would cook, clean and fuss but she didn't mean any harm. She was funny and I felt like I had a mom but when she would be in need of a high, she was someone else. I was always going out to this club called Sneakers. It was a teenage club we would all go to and I had a few friends that lived around the corner that I would hang with all the time and became real close with so we would go out together. I was always on the go so much to where nothing bothered me. We were about to go the club one night and for some reason I haven't started my period so I was telling my friend and her sister had a pregnancy test and she went to get it for me and I took it and it came back positive. I really didn't think much of it and still went out. I didn't drink or smoke I was just hanging out a lot and getting into fights. At the age of fifteen, I was pregnant and didn't realize I was about to be a mom until I started feeling the baby move. I was going to the Dr. but I did it because it was the thing to do, not because I cared much of having a baby but because I knew I didn't know what to do with a baby at sixteen.

I have this baby; I wanted to give her up for an adoption. I never had plans for having kids. I didn't want kids but my plans were not God's plans. I told my mom and she didn't believe me because I was so small and I didn't sleep a lot. I was always an eater so she never noticed when my eating became more or less. I continued to hang out in the streets with my friends so my life style didn't change much. As soon as I told her I started getting big and sleeping a lot. I was still going to school but after lunch I had Government class and I would sleep the whole class through. I didn't miss a beat of school because it had hit me that I would have a baby to take care of and I had to finish high school. My mom wasn't that supportive. She would ask if I had a Dr. Apt but she never went with me. I would always go by myself. On my six-teenth birthday I was watching the Cosby Show eating roman noodles with cheese and hot sauce and I was thinking, "Wow I'm sixteen, pregnant, and big as ever what a way to spend my sixteenth birthday". But it was okay because it was hot and I was about to have this baby next month and I was going to be back to myself, or so I thought.

It was the summer of 1994 and my cousins from Minnesota would come down and stay with my aunt (their grandmother), I was pregnant but I would still try to hang. So when they came I went to hang out with them at my aunt's house. Now by this time I'm ready to pop, running around the apartment complex having water balloon fights and for some reason it was feeling like I had either urinated on myself or it was my clothes that were wet. My aunt was yelling at me telling me to sit down before my water brake. I went to change my clothes and layed down and for some reason it still felt like I was leaking fluid. I let my aunt know, she called my mom, and we went to the hospital. After sitting in the hospital for hours they said it wasn't my water and I could go home. Drink plenty of fluids and rest. I knew something was not right and I was just ready to have this baby. When I got home my little brother and I walked around the neighborhood and I had the big cup they gave me from the hospital full of water, so as I walked he was riding his bike. No matter where I was or went, my baby brother was right there with me. I walked until I couldn't walk anymore.

When I got home, I took a shower and washed my hair because a friend of mine that was living with us was going to braid my hair for me because it wasn't going to be long before I would go into the hospital to deliver my baby girl and I didn't want my hair to be all over my head. As I came down the stairs I could smell my momma cooking spaghetti, garlic bread, and salad. I was so hungry, tired, my baby was putting her feet or hands in my ribs, I couldn't tell the difference I just knew it hurt and I hated when she did that, and I just wanted to eat and lay down. As soon as I sat down what do you know, my water broke. It felt like as if my bladder had popped. When I tell you everybody ran around the house except me. I wasn't hurting so I wanted to eat and besides my hair wasn't done. My momma was happier than I was. She rushed me into the car and was speeding to get me to the hospital.

As we arrived to the hospital and I was still not in pain. I was thinking this does not hurt I have no idea what people was talking about. But of course I didn't know what I was supposed to feel anyway. I was sixteen, having a baby. When they got me to a room and I started hearing the screaming from other women having babies; I started getting nervous. I was thinking, "Ok, I'm ready to give this back I'm not ready for all this." But I realize this wasn't a situation I could just give back and be done with. It didn't work like that. After six hours of Labor and smelling Long John Silver's in my room; On July 3,1994, I gave birth to a very healthy, head full of hair, 6lb 6oz and 19 ½-inch long baby girl. This is when it got real for me. I'm a mother now.

Chapter 7

A BABY HAVING A BABY

1 Thessalonians 5:18 *give thanks in all circumstances; for this is God's will for you in Christ Jesus.*

As I sat in the hospital bed looking at this baby that I just gave birth to, I had no idea what to do with her, I was numb. I didn't have a job or a dime. I didn't think about the fact that I had to buy diapers, wipes, clothes, shoes, socks, medicine, etc. I didn't feel like I loved this baby like I should have because I didn't know how to love another human being, I didn't know how a mother was supposed to love her child, all I could think of was, "Is it too late for adoption?" Now, her father and I were not in a relationship. Did I like him? A little but not enough to have a baby for him. I was still a baby, 15 was not old enough to know what I wanted and sure not old enough to have a baby, I was way too wild for that. He was older than me and he had a daughter already so he knew how this thing was supposed to go. Throughout my pregnancy I really didn't want to have anything to do with him. So after I delivered he was informed that I had the baby. OMG, THIS CHILD LOOKS JUST LIKE THIS MAN!!!!!!!!! He helped out a little but not a lot but I didn't really ask him for much anyway.

It was the Fourth of July and I was going home. I lost all that weight and I was ready to hit the streets again. But wait a minute. What am I going to do with the baby? Oh well, she can go too. I wasn't letting that slow me down. I would leave her with my mom when I would go to school but later that wasn't safe to do. School started in August and I was a Jr in High school with a baby. While I was in school I was being told I could go to an alternative school with girls who have babies and I refused to go. I'm going to school and graduate just like any other student. I was the type of kid that thrived off of a challenge. I felt like it was a challenge to tell me to go to an alternative school as if I couldn't do as other students because I had a baby. Now It's the first day of school and some friends and I decided to leave and hang out in Rock Island, it's just the first day of school what are we going to really miss anyway? This is where the bad boys were and because we lived in Bettendorf and none of them where there we would go to where they were. We pulled up to some guys that were on the corner. My friend that was driving at the time, one of the boys was her boyfriend or a guy friend of hers, but the rest of us just went to hang out. There was this boy that was standing there on the corner, just looking just how I liked, a roughkneck. He was dark, short and looked like he may have had his hair in braids and had just took them down because it had that crinkle look; he was wearing a white- t shirt and some jeans. He looked like he knew what he wanted and was just minding his own buisness. I got his attention by saying something real slick and he came back with a slick one on me, so after that I asked him for his number and he gave it to me but not on paper. He gave it to me verbally and fast as if he didn't want me to have it, but I was a fast learner so I caught it really quick.

I called him but he was always acting like he was busy or was leaving to go somewhere. It was ok with me because I was moving around too. After a while, we started talking and started seeing each other more. We never said we were in a relationship; we just had a connection that was unexplainable. Shortly thereafter, I brought my daughter around and it almost looked like we were a family. He took on to her like she was his. This wasn't that kind of relationship, he was more like my friend than my boyfriend but we didn't have to explain our place with each other because we knew where we stood with each other.

I didn't have to have a babysitter because my mom would keep Day while I was at school. As time went on, my mom was getting to where her addiction was getting to the point where she had to have it and she would take my baby with her when she would get high. This is when it got real for me; I was not going to allow this. I didn't want my daughter brought up like this and I was not going to allow anybody to come between me and my daughter; I was a fighter about mine. I came home and my mom had taken my daughter and was gone all day; I couldn't find her and I started getting worried because I didn't know where she was. I later found her at the drug house. Right then, I decided I'm not staying in this house with my mom anymore. I was not going to just let my baby be around those types of people because they were destroying my family, but at the same time I was into those types of boys. I know, crazy, right? But that was all I knew. But didn't want it for my baby.

I pretty much was unstable for a while, living with person to person and I learned you can only live with people for so long before they will get tired of you and talk about you and then treat you like they were ready for you to go. But through it all, it was always me and my baby. I was not happy not having her in her own space. Everywhere I went was hurtful to me because I didn't want to pack my daughter from place to place. I lived with family and my cousin was there to help me also. She would watch my daughter while I went to school and she would take me to school. She had three kids of her own as a single mother and I just felt like it was too much for me to be there with my baby so I moved in with another friend. I never had a stable life but one person that was stable was God because through it all he kept me when I didn't have enough sense to keep myself.

I had no stability in my life; I was all over the place trying to find myself. I later got my own apartment and I was excited. Now I remind you, I didn't have a job, so I was on welfare. I was getting $361 a month and I paid rent, electric, toiletries, shoes, and clothes. I had to wash at the laundry mat so this went fast, but I did what I could to make it. Quincy helped until he went to jail. I was determined to make a liar out of those who said I wasn't going to finish high school and be nothing. I was able to go to school but was an independent student, so I could only miss a certain amount of days of school. I missed only for the days I had a Dr. appt. for my daughter, if she was sick, or DHS appt, which was not often but it was hard to try not to go over. The daycare that my daughter had went to had a bus that would pick me up from my apartment and to take us to the daycare to drop her off; take me to school, pick me up from school, pick her up from daycare, and take us home so there was no excuses why I could go to school.

I never was one to have a lot of company at my house, just a few friends but didn't make my house the hang out spot. I got up to go to school everyday. The only time I would miss was due to my daughter being sick or something important. So when my baby got sick and I couldn't find anyone to watch her it was really disappointing to me. She couldn't go to the daycare and my thoughts were, "What am I going to do? I can't miss much more of school." I was home with her a few days and was dropped from school. I was devastated. I cried and felt like I let my baby down because she deserved that much from me to finish high school and not give up and I couldn't seem to do that. I felt like I couldn't do anything right at that point. I called my grandma, crying my eyes out. "I Can't DO THIS I WANT TO FINISH SCHOOL AND NOW I CAN'T." She said, "I'm going to send you a train ticket and you get on that train and get here so you can finish." I had a ticket in the next two days to Oakland, California.

Don't get me wrong, it may have been people who were willing to help me but I didn't trust anyone so I didn't give anyone the chance. All I trusted were my grandma and my aunt. That's it. So, as the word got back to my mom her and my aunt came over, trying to talk me into staying but they never said what they would and could do to help me but I wasn't mad because this was my child and I couldn't be mad when no one wanted to help. My mind was made up and I was leaving. When the day came for me to leave, my good friend Nicole took me to the train station in Galesburg, Illinois. I really was going to miss her, she and her family had been so good to me and they did not judge me because I had a baby.

Chapter 8

REFUSED TO BE A STATISTIC

> **Matthew 7:7-8** 7 *"Ask and it will be given to you; seek and you will find; knock and the door will be opened to you. 8 For everyone who asks receives; the one who seeks finds; and to the one who knocks, the door will be opened."*

As my baby girl and I got on the train, I had so much on my mind. What was I doing, where did I go wrong, and what does this mean? I asked God, what was he telling me, but at seventeen and not knowing how to hear from God it was just silent because I was waiting to hear a voice and all I got was silence. I didn't know if he was speaking back or if I was crazy talking to someone who does not even exist. I didn't know his voice, the Word or his work, I just knew "God, help me" and only knew that from asking that so much when I was younger.

As I looked out the window all I saw was green, and mountains that were so big, some far away some very close I felt as if I could touch them. As I think about it now that's how life is. There are mountains we have to climb that are close that we are climbing now and then there are those that are far away that we will soon have to climb. I was thinking, "How can I just get there, far away to sit high and look low." As I'm lost in my own thoughts, I hear my baby in the background saying, "MOMMY LOOK" as she pointed out the window to the same mountains I was looking at, smiling, looking so happy without a care in the world. It's amazing how happy kids can be during hard times. Me not knowing that those same mountains that I'm climbing will be the same mountains she will have to one day climb also. So we walked on the train, watched TV and I let her run through the aisles a little bit because there wasn't a lot of people on the train at that time. That was the longest almost three-day ride ever. I couldn't wait to touch water because a wash up can only go so far. When I arrived in Oakland, I was so happy and was ready to see my family.

As we were coming into Oakland, I looked out the window at the freeway where the earthquake had destroyed it. It hadn't been fixed yet. It was terrible. Just thinking of all the people that may had lost their lives; I was just hoping I didn't have to experience that while I was here. As I got off the train I saw my aunt and cousin. I was so happy to see them and they were just as happy to see me and Day. My aunt and Day were so happy to see each other like they had seen each other before. I had cut all my hair off before I left so when I got there I was thinking, "Are people going to look at me like I'm crazy because I don't have any hair?" When we got to the house, it was a building with different apartments in it, my aunt lived down stairs and my grandma lived upstairs, both were studio apartments but we were all family and I was happy with that.

My aunt took me to enroll in school and I was excited. Since it was so close to the end of the school year, I didn't have enough credits to graduate because I had missed a semester and a half and I had to go to summer school and ended up graduating in '97. That was fine with me as long as

I graduated out of high school and didn't have to go to any alternative schools or get my GED; '97 it will be. I didn't feel bad that my hair was cut off because I guess that was the style at that time. I have a pretty good grade of hair so all I had to do to it was water and pink lotion on my hair and go I just needed some big hoops; well I thought so. My first day of school and I'm looking at everyone and the girls were dressed cute with short shorts, skirts, half shirts, and cute sandals. I was thinking, "I need some clothes." My clothes were a no go. I looked like a little boy. Jeans, T- shirts, and tennis shoes.

When I got home and I went down stairs to talk to my aunt and we were laughing because I was telling her I needed some clothes; I looked like a little boy because these jeans and t-shirts were not going to work. It was bad enough when I opened my mouth, people couldn't understand what I was saying because of my Southern accent, but to dress country? OMG, I stuck out like a sore thumb. I started getting some money coming in so I started going shopping and the clothes were cheap. I would go to the flea market on E 14th because it was close to me and I could walk there and I was small too, so that made my shopping easier.

My first day of summer school at Fremont, which was my home school and I have no friends really from school yet but it's okay because my focus was on trying to get done. There was this one girl there and we seem to be by ourselves a lot anyway. We started talking and she went to Castlemont High. We started talking and hanging out and she started showing me around and how to catch the bus and after that it was on. We became very close and may I add we still talk today. I call her my first Oakland best friend. We ended up being really close friends. There was another girl that was very cool with us and it was just the three of us and we kicked it all summer long and afterwards. We didn't have to have any-thing planned but when we got done sitting and talking we ended up having fun without having spent a dime or planning anything in advance. We caught the bus everywhere. Shy loved her long nails; that was something I just couldn't do but that was her thing and that's what made her special because she had her own unique thing about herself and I had mine but we never looked down on each other about them. She had a great family they were very open to me and invited me and my daughter in with open arms without a question.

Man, it's my senior year and there was no stopping me now. I'm about to be done with high school and on to my next journey to take care of my baby girl. I worked at Wendy's while in school, ran track and still made time for my baby and to study. Now I have two other friends that I just can't explain my feelings for them. All I can say is, I think we were supposed to be triplets because they are twins. I tell you God has sent some of the best people in my life. We did everything together. If I fell asleep at their house, I could. If one didn't have, we made it to where everybody had. If one ate, we all ate. We had our fallouts but they didn't last. I love my twins.

After I graduated, I was thinking what to do now. Its graduation day and I'm super excited, my friends are there, my grandma and aunt was there and I was extremely happy to see their faces.. As I looked through the crowd of people I spotted my grandma and she was watching, I was so happy. As I walked across the stage, I looked up at my grandma, waved at her and as I exited the stage, she was leaving. My grandma is a very straight forward person. She came to see me walk then she left; that's all I wanted her to see anyway. To see me complete. My aunt had flowers and balloons for me but I was so on the go I got them when I got home but it meant so much to me that those two showed up and my daughter was right there. That's all that really mattered.

I had no clue of what I wanted to do but I knew it was in the medical field. My track coach and his wife stayed in my ear about me taking a scholarship to Grambling but I refused to take it because I had my baby and didn't have anyone to care for her. I was very picky with who I left her with so I went and enrolled myself into a Vo Tech school that was very expensive but I didn't get the advisement that I needed for college, so I didn't finish. Not that I didn't want to finish; I just didn't know where I wanted to go or do. I just knew I needed to take care of my daughter. I had the drive but just not the push. I knew I didn't want to work at Wendy's or Merritt Bakery the rest of my life and I also knew I wanted to be successful because of what I was told before. It wasn't to prove a point to those who said I cant but to prove that I can. Somewhere between after I graduated from high school and me trying to find myself me and the twins started going to church together. This was when I started searching for God on my own.

Shortly after I graduated, I got my own apartment but I never really stayed there. I was still at my grandmas all the time. She didn't want me to move but I knew if I ever needed to go back home I could with no question asked. Because I figured she had taken care of us long enough and I had said that after I finish high school I was going to go back and get my own place but I was at her house everyday anyway and she didn't complain at all. I applied for Housing and I was housed in some apartments behind the Oakland Coliseum and the BART station, which were considered to be the Projects. I could hear when there was a football game; I could hear the BART train but the public transportation was great where I was located since I didn't have a car. I didn't like the place, once I saw a mouse; I was pretty much done. I wanted to go back and stay with my grandma but my pride didn't let me ask her. I didn't know God was working his plan out for me. I was going to church but really didn't understand who God was and what his work was about. All I knew was when I got something good it was God. I didn't know that when things turned for bad that could be Him also.

So I went and got me a car. My first good running car a white '94 Ford Tempo. I was excited. My baby and I were rolling then. But I still wasn't happy. One day I pulled up at my grandma's house and I was outside talking to my little cousins and some other friends from the neighborhood and my grandma always knew when I was around for some reason like she could smell me or something and she yelled out the backdoor, "TOOT YOU OUT THERE?" I said, "YES", Now I was trying to figure out how she knew I was outside because I hadn't even went in the house yet I just pulled up and started talking to my little cousin. But knowing my grandma she watched everything about us she didn't miss a beat. she said your momma on the phone, come talk to her. I had an attitude because I didn't want to talk to her. I didn't feel like my day being messed up by her asking me a bunch of questions. But my grandma gave me that look and said, "Get yo butt on that phone and stop acting like that" so I straightened up really quick.

As I got on the phone, my grandma left the room and I was alone, just me, the phone and my mom on the other line. She was talking like she was not on anything. She told me she had been to rehab and wanted to try to have her kids back together. I thought about it and I wanted to be with my mom also but I could not take dealing with the drugs and her behavior with the drugs because it made me hate her. Because she said she was trying, I agreed to go back to the Quad City Area with her and my brothers. When she sent me a bus ticket to leave, I told my grandma and aunt I was leaving and they were hurt I could tell, but they also wanted me to be with my mom also. I pretty much sold everything in my apartment and stayed with my grandma until I left. My grandma told me if I wanted to come back let her know and I could.

When the day came for me to leave, I said my goodbyes to my grandma and she cried, I cried but she said call me when you get there. I didn't want to leave my family in California and my friends, but my mom wanted her family back together and I wanted my mother's love. I had my grandmother's love and my aunties love but I didn't have my mother's love and I was hungry for it. I thought about a lot on this long bus ride. I thought about all the traveling I've done with me and my baby trying to find happiness and couldn't seem to be settled anywhere. I thought about how much I loved my grandma and how me going between the both of them was not good for nobody. But I wanted to be in my mom life I wanted to feel the love from her as I felt from my Aunt and my grandma. I knew she loved me but what kind of love was it that she was giving me. So she said she changed and want her kids all back together. Well it has been a while and maybe she is for real because I want my daughter to know her grandma like I knew mine.

Chapter 9

ANOTHER LET DOWN

As I arrived, I wasn't all that excited; something just wasn't right. Something in my spirit just didn't let me feel free. As I got off the bus and I saw my mom and little brothers, I started feeling like, "Ok maybe she was for real about her change." When my mom dropped us off at the house she said she would be right back and that right back turned into one week. Well ain't this some mess, whatever that feeling was that I had on that bus as I arrived in the Quad City Area it was a real feeling telling me "Don't come back here it's about to be some mess" My brothers were doing whatever they wanted to do; they had kids coming in and out all day and night from the front door to the back door. My thoughts were "OH HELL, NAW, I COULD'VE STAYED IN OAKLAND FOR THIS MESS, AINT NOTHING CHANGED."

I had a few hundred dollars in my pocket and I wanted to get a ticket to get the hell out of there, but I felt like my brothers needed me, so I stayed and I went and found a job. I was able to get a job in the Casino working in the restaurant and was able to start saving for my own apartment. I got me a car and put my daughter in daycare. Even though I lived with my mom, it was hard to live with her during her time of using. It was crazy. There was no order at all, again; I'm on my own, no help and I didn't want to tell my grandma because she would have went crazy and her and my momma would have got into it so I stuck it out until I got my own place. When I did move she was upset, she didn't understand why I wanted to move and pay someone else rent instead of paying her and staying at home to help her.

I was tired of hearing things were different and they weren't. I got tired of going backwards. I wanted better for my daughter and me. I didn't want her to have to grow up to see this kind of stuff. So I moved. The apartments were based on my income, a two bedroom, very clean and neat area, all bills paid, and a great school district. I was excited when I got my keys. We slept on the floor for a few weeks but we were ok. It was my own apartment and my daughter had her own room and space. I got enrolled in school for a few classes and was working, so I guess I was getting on the right path.

I was sitting at home watching TV by myself because Day was spending time at my mom's house, so I thought about Quincy mom and called to see how she was doing. She answered the phone and I was a little surprised when she said somebody is here hold on and this deep voice got on the phone that made my heart drop to the floor because I wasn't expecting to hear his voice. It was Quincy. I couldn't stop smiling on the other end of the phone. I felt a glow on my face and throughout my body. I was so excited, all I could say was, "I'm on my way to see you." I jumped up and was looking for my keys and couldn't find them fast enough because I was so nervous. When I found them I didn't even change my clothes, I went in my PJ's and house shoes. You would have thought my little Geo Prizm had wings. I flew across that bridge as fast as I could to see him. The closer I got, the more nervous I got. As I pulled up in the driveway my heart was beating out of my chest, my hands were sweating, my nerves were shook. It has been so long since I seen him I didn't know how I was going to react.

I knocked on the door and I heard "come in." When I walked in the house his mom and aunt were in the dining room talking and she called him from the basement to come upstairs. I was so excited to see him. It was like me seeing my best friend all over again. We sat down in the living room and we talked for a while and all of a sudden a girl came from the basement walking through the living room out the front door. (1st red flag.) I shook my head and said, "Same ole Quincy" and laughed in my head, it couldn't be me.

I knew where we stood with each other before so it wasn't a doubt in my mind that he would disrespect me in that order ever. He did have other flings before but I never saw it. I felt as he respected me enough not to do it in my face. We knew what each other was doing but we knew our place with each other also because I wasn't any angel either. We were both young and were being young. As she left he showed no sign of caring much (2nd red flag.), which I didn't care because I had my man back and I wasn't going to let anything get in the way this time so I sat back and just watched. With what I saw I didn't have to do much but sit still and be quiet. He made the decision without a question on where he wanted to be and that was with me.

We were always going to be friends anyway, so that was something no one could take away. As she left I felt some-what bad but then again, I felt like, "Good, go on girl, because there is not enough room for three on this ride anyway. This ride is for two, max." We sat and talked for hours. It was like a conversation that just flowed. No pause in it. We laughed, joked and just had good company with each other without being scared, ashamed or trying to win him over because we already knew the good, the bad, and ugly of each other, so there was nothing to hide. When it started to get late, we said our good nights and I went home. I felt so good on the inside like I have been complete. I felt like the piece that was missing is now together. I have never thought I could trust a man and put my all into one like I did him. I felt like I had exhaled.

Because he was on house arrest, I had to go see him and I did every day, all day. When I would get off work I was there with him. I didn't have a problem with it at all; that is where I wanted to be and that was where I was going to be, right there with him until he comes home. I couldn't wait until Fridays when I got off work to spend my Friday nights with him watching movies; me, him and Day. It would be pretty late when I would go home but as soon as I woke up, I was right there with him all day, all night so I pretty much knew who was coming over to visit so I wasn't even worried about him cheating on me because he made me feel secure about our relationship.

As I was lying around most of the day, I wasn't feeling too good. I was feeling like I was coming down with a cold or something. My body was feeling really weak and I was feeling nauseous. It was getting late and I just wanted to lie down and sleep. Quincy saw something was wrong so he thought I should go to the ER. I got there feeling weak. They asked me numerous of questions and one of them was, "Are you pregnant?" I told her NO with the look of death because I was not having any more kids and didn't want any more kids and that was not part of my plan. (If you want to make God laugh, tell him your plans.)

The Nurse came in and wanted to draw some lab work on me. I was fine with that because I was tired and wanted to get over whatever it was I had. After she drew my lab work, I laid in the bed looking up at the ceiling trying to figure out if it was something I may had ate, or if I was around anyone that was sick. There was a knock at the door, "Miss Jackson?" Yes? "I have your results from your labs. Remember when I asked you if you could be pregnant?" I didn't even reply, again I gave her the look of death, the one when my left eyebrow goes up and I just stare. "Well, you're pregnant." For that moment everything stopped. My heart, blood pressure, and my world. I asked her for another test because clearly she had the wrong results for the wrong patient. At that point the Dr. came in and I asked, "How far am I?" He did a pap and he said because I was so early it was hard to tell but maybe about 3-4 weeks. I was thinking this is going to be a long pregnancy. Very early, too early to know now I was thinking.

When they left the room, I cleaned myself up and called Quincy from the ER. I told him I was pregnant. I could hear the happiness through the phone from him as it was silent because he wanted me to have his child for some time now. So I went back over to his house and I was not happy about the situation at all but he was so happy he smiled the whole time rubbing my stomach calling it his son already. The joy of him being happy later on made me happy. I knew he was going to be a great father but one thing we never discussed was being married. I didn't feel like I was going to be alone during this pregnancy, he was with me every step of the way from the beginning to the end. It became the perfect pregnancy a woman could ask for. I got kisses and I love you all the time. Often If I was hungry he fed me; if my back hurt he rubbed it, if my feet hurt he rubbed them, if I wanted to rest he laid with me. There was nothing I asked for that I didn't get.

I knew without a doubt we were going to be together forever, there was nothing that could break this. I went to visit my good friend that I've been friends with for some years now. As we are sitting back talking, she brings up a statement about Quincy. I've never been one to just believe what a dude tells me because I know they be lying but I've also have had friends that lied, also it's kind of hard to believe anything that anybody would say so she goes to tell me that my baby daddy has another baby on the way. By this time, I'm about three months along and I had to question that statement because I was with him everyday all day except when I was at work, so I know he didn't have time to make a baby with someone else.

So I ask by whom? She said "By a girl who works with my cousin's baby momma." You know I'm mad and want answers cause I'm trying to figure out how, when, and why? As we finished talking, I went across the bridge to see him. I'm driving and I'm thinking, this can't be true this has to be a lie, because I'm with him all day everyday and late at night so where does he have time to do anything like this? As I pulled up to the house I'm really mad and can't believe the news I just got so I sit down in the front room and he looked at me and could tell something was going on so he asked me," What's wrong boo?" I asked him, "Do you have another baby on the way?" He gave me this look like, where would you get that from? He says, "No, how am I going to have another baby when you're here every day and night?" Right; my same question and since I never had any run-ins with no other females over to his house or with him on the phone I really didn't have any reason to doubt what he was saying was true but I'm not crazy either. Innocent until proven guilty.

Chapter 10

DADDY'S HOME

I'm loving my life right now. My man is home; we are officially a family now. He makes sure I'm not stressed or unhappy. I'm loving him more and more every day. He is making this pregnant thing the greatest thing ever. There is nothing like having the father of your unborn child there to rub your stomach and your back and to watch your stomach grow with his child in it. To have him to talk to his baby, watch and feel his baby move, and for his baby to hear his daddy's voice was one of the best things a woman could have and I wasn't giving that up for anything.

I'm not going to lie; I didn't want any more kids. I had mixed emotions about this pregnancy in the beginning but as time progressed and to see the joy and glow in him; I to begin to have the same joy and glow. I knew he was going to be a great daddy because he was a great daddy to my daughter. We met when she was a month old and there was nothing he wouldn't do for her. Not only was he good to her but his family was too. Treated her just like their own, so he showed me he was going to be the father that our son needed. Before I knew what I was having, his mom had bought so many clothes and things for this baby; he was spoiled before he had his sex gender appeared. He was a much-loved baby from His uncles, friends and family. I can honestly say he didn't want for anything and neither did I.

We're home, its good but then he started leaving a little more but he always stayed in touch with home, making sure I was ok I understood he was gone for a while and wanted to hang out with his friends and get back to himself so I didn't trip about it. He made sure home was taken care of and I had no worries. In fact, I was able to stop working sooner than I planned so I could rest and not stress about bills etc. I start having these weird dreams about me knocking on a door and he opens the door holding a baby girl. Around this time, Mary J's album "Mary" came out and "It's your child" was a song that I loved. I don't know why but I did and I played it all the time but never thought much about it. I'm a big Mary J fan so at the time I had all her CD's. She kept me on my game. His being gone was not an issue to me as some may have thought it was and those are the ones that knew what was going on and didn't tell me. I wouldn't say I was being naïve, I just didn't know. It was covered very well.

I slept all day, my body was just tired and when I finally got comfortable to where I could sleep, I was out. Day was a great kid she didn't bother me, she stayed in her room watching TV or playing with her toys. I heard a knock on the door but I didn't move. I ignored it until they knocked again and Day came to my room to tell me someone was knocking on the door. I got up with an attitude because they had no idea what it took for me to even get to sleep. It was Girl Scouts selling cookies. I was so mad, so I said," NO I DON'T AND PLEASE DON'T KNOCK ON MY DOOR LIKE THAT AGAIN!!!!"

Well since I was up and it was nice out, the sun was shining so Day and I got up, took showers and went across the bridge to visit my baby boy grandma. As we pulled up I wobbled my way to the front door as I was saying to myself, "I wish this baby would come today, ugh." Sitting in the chair

I always sat in seem to be very uncomfortable this day. My back was killing me and I couldn't sit still. I wasn't feeling right so his mom called him to come check on me. Instead of him coming to get me from her house I wanted to try to make it home. As I was driving home, my lower back was hurting more and more. I pulled up to the house and I was in the most unbearable pain to where I had to crawl to the front door and Day had to unlock the front door for me.

By then all I could do is lay in the middle of the floor in a ball trying not to cry because I didn't want to scare my baby. She stood over me asking if I was ok but I couldn't tell a five year old I was ok on the floor in a ball. I covered my tears and told her the baby is in a different position and I'm trying to get him comfortable. Shortly after Quincy walked in scared as ever not knowing what to do. I wanted to go to the hospital and he wanted to call the Dr. She told him to run me some bath water but I was not trying to hear that; I couldn't walk how am I going to get in the bath tub. When he realized I was in pain he started looking for his car keys that he never came in the house with. We go to the car and the car is still running. We get in the car and it smelled just like gas. I didn't know if I wanted to die because of the pain I was in or because the smell of gas was choking me, either way I needed to get to the hospital.

I didn't know what to expect because I didn't have this kind of pain with my daughter so I didn't know what was wrong. I knew it had to have something to do with having the baby but does it hurt like this? As we got to the hospital, I'm thinking I'm about to have the baby soon with all this pain and not realizing my water haven't broke yet. Ok, so what am I waiting for? Come on baby; break the water so you can give mommy a break? That was not happening, so I walked around the hospital with his uncle for a little and then I was sent back to the room to bounce on a ball because this baby wasn't down far enough. With his family there it made me feel the love and support of knowing that I wasn't going to have to do this alone.

As it got late, my Dr. confirmed that I was in labor and she was keeping me over night. He stayed there with me until I went to sleep and he took Day home to get her ready for school the next day. I was so out of it I went straight to sleep. The next day came, no baby still and my water hadn't broken either. My Dr. came in tell me she can break my water to get started but I didn't want to do it until Quincy got there. I called him to tell him they are breaking my water at ten and he was excited he didn't want me doing it without him there so he hurried to take Day to his mom because it was spring break and we didn't have any one else to keep her.

He made it before ten and as the water broke, it was time to get this going. He was there with me the whole time by my side as he said he would be. This was so hard for me I wanted to have a c-section, the pain was unbearable. I got in the whirlpool and that seem to hurt more and he got in with me. I was like a whale in that pool. Water was hitting my side and I just couldn't take it. When I came to the hospital it was dark, now it's dark again so you mean to tell me I been here in this hospital for twenty-four hrs. I'm saying aloud, "I'm never having any more kids this is it." My body was tired, my mind was tired; I didn't go through this with my daughter she was six hrs and done so what is this all about?

As I was resting, I heard my mom's voice. She had the most irritating voice but you could not miss it."COME ON GRANDMA, POO HEAD COME ON OUT OF THERE" and when she said that contractions started going all I could do is tell her to be quiet and she didn't they kept coming. I was feeling more pressure and when I got checked my Dr. said it could be a few more hours. LORD HELP I CANT DO THIS ANOTHER HOUR!!!!!!Quincy and my mom were there and the Dr. informed them it would be a little while longer so they stepped out and I was lying there by myself.

As soon as they left about ten minutes later, I was feeling some pressure as if I was sitting on something. I called the Nurses to tell them I think I'm sitting on my baby's head and she came in moving really slow as if didn't know what I was talking about. As she came in I was sitting up on my hands because I was sitting on his head. I asked her to hurry up because he was coming out and she said, "It may just be pressure." As she lifted the sheet up, I was looking at her and the look on her face was as she seen a ghost. She said, "DON'T PUSH IT'S THE BABY HEAD" and she rushed to get the crew to deliver and everyone was running in and I couldn't wait for them he just came out. I was so happy; man my body felt like a big weight had been lifted off me. But I didn't hear any cry. Where was my baby? He was just blue; he was short of oxygen but thank God for His mercy and Grace. Quincy was so happy the look on his face was indescribable. He was so happy and he had fell in love with this little boy.

Its time to go home and the first night at home, baby would not stop crying. We rocked him, changed his diaper and did all we could to find out what was wrong. I was tired and Quincy was also. We took turns being up with him. Quincy got up with him, rocked him, talked to him, and even drove him in the car. Finally he went to sleep. I called his grandma the next day to tell her he showed out and she said, "Give him some cereal, that baby hungry." I didn't have any so I made some cream of wheat and put it in his bottle and he slept like the baby he was.

The next day, Quincy left and didn't come home for a few days. At this time I thought he would be home more with us or inform me where he was going and where he was going to be. I guess having the baby didn't change for him but it did for me. As I found out, you can't allow something to go on for so long and when you're tired everything will change. That's not the case. Just because now I'm ready for him to be home doesn't mean he's ready. I allowed by him to go and come as he pleased without laying any grounds down because I was ok, but now I have two babies and want him around more. He's not ready and now we have a problem. I had the baby you wanted and now you're never home with us.

I couldn't get him to touch me anymore, the sex had stopped and I'm noticing a big change in his attitude with me. He didn't want to have sex with me when I was pregnant because he said he didn't want to hurt the baby. Now the baby is here, I can't get you to even kiss me. Something is wrong, having this baby just ruined my relationship but I loved my baby and was feeling like I was torn between the two. I asked him why he didn't want to have sex with me anymore and he told me because he didn't realize how wide my vagina opened up and it was a turn off. I felt so ashamed, disappointed and a failure. I didn't understand because when we met, I had a baby one month before but we didn't have sex until about three months. I tried to understand but couldn't.

Chapter 11

IT'S TIME TO GO

Ecclesiastes 3:6 *a time to search and a time to give up, a time to keep and a time to throw away.*

S itting at my mom's house talking to her with the baby and Day; I called my son's dad to remind him of the car insurance that needed to be paid. He said ok, he was on his way to bring me the money. As he got there he came in the house and I came down stairs to meet him. He hadn't been home in days; he was supposed to be out of town so I wasn't tripping. As we were talking and he handed me the money, I noticed he had hospital band on. I'm confused because his band from the hospital was at the house so I said, "Are you ok? You've been to the hospital, why do you have a band on?"

He pulled his hand back from me in a way as if he didn't want me to see the band and kept telling me it was nothing. Finally I saw it. It had teddy bears on it with BG and the mother's last name was on it. My heart immediately hit the bottom of my feet. I felt a pain in my stomach that took my breath away. As I looked him in his eyes, I know him; I knew he was lying and he couldn't find anything to say to me. Everything started replaying back to me from the beginning of me first finding out that this girl was pregnant to the dreams I was having to the song I was listing to and the always gone. I trusted him. Never trusted anyone like I trusted him. That trust was easily broken and there was nothing that could change it at this point.

After the baby, everything started coming out, the other women, and his staying gone more. As I talked to others they would tell me, "That is his baby and if you're going to continue to be with him, you have to deal with his baby." Although my heart was broken, I still tried to make it work but in my heart, I wanted to be done. I was not wanting this relationship anymore. It started getting worse, not better. I didn't try anymore because I didn't care. I just wanted away. He was my best friend. He understood me and never judged me of anything I did or what I went through. I wanted my family back but there was no trust and I didn't want to deal with a baby that was made from him cheating on me.

So I did what I thought he wanted, for us to make it work. I started going to go get the baby even though I didn't want to. I did it because I wanted my family back so I thought if he saw that I was ok, he would be home more and be willing to do better with us, but deep down it was fake. I didn't want to deal with the baby but I never mistreated the baby. As time went on that wasn't the case anymore, he had another woman so I was done with the whole situation. I had no energy anymore, I was ready to go. I didn't want to be there anymore. Even though I didn't know how to pray; I was asking God, "What am I to do?" This was a lot for me to deal with. I was hurt, torn apart, my trust was gone and nothing was left but my kids and me. I was trying to figure out how everyone knew about all this that was going on all this time and didn't say a word to me about any of it. The trust that I had with those who knew was out the window. How can you know something so important and still have the nerve to talk and go on with someone like nothing was wrong?

I was trying so hard to brush the whole thing under the rug, but deep down I was broken to pieces, broken to the point the pieces were shattered and couldn't be found to even try to tape them back together. I didn't have anyone to talk to. This was a time I needed my mom. I needed to cry and ask her how does this work. I needed so much support because I was lost. The ones that I did trust and thought I could go to were the ones who knew what was going on, so there was no need to even go to them with my hurt. I was left alone to figure this thing out but I was not going to allow it to kill me to where I couldn't take care of my children. The more I asked God for understanding the more it started being clear to me that it was time to go. I was missing my grandmother anyway. I had family here but nothing took the place of my grandma.

I got to thinking; I had left California to make things right with my mom and it wasn't. Then I ended up with another baby that I didn't want to have. I had loved this man so much, he didn't have any kids and I knew we were going to be together. He played the role of a good dad to my daughter. He was there for us so I gave in and gave him a son because I knew we were going to be together for ever. This man that I love with all in me had betrayed me to the max. That was my best friend. I thought we could tell each other anything. I lost my best friend and at that point it was time to go. I quit my job; I called my friend and told her I was coming, printed out a map, packed what clothes I could fit in my car for me and my kids, got in my car and left. I thought Lord, where do I go from here? I didn't have a plan. I didn't have a job lined up, or a place to live. I had about $500 in my pocket and I just up and went.

I didn't go to a place that I looked up. I went back to the place that caused me more pain and could have killed me. You ask, why go back? I asked the same question. Because I didn't know His voice or know how to have a relationship with Him as I do now. He was telling me to go get my life back. I was being obedient and didn't know it. I'm not where I want to be but I am in a peaceful place with God now. I know how to hear from Him, I know how to rest in his arms, and the best thing is I know whose I am. I don't always do right but he always seem to come through at my breaking points. To know his voice now is such a sweet sound to my ear. I look at all the things that could've broke me to pieces but because of his Grace and Mercy brought me through. His agape love for me is beyond what even I can understand

ACKNOWLEDGMENTS

G iving honor to God, my Lord Jesus Christ, who is the head of my life; foundation, health, wealth, mind, body and soul. I want to thank you for being a shield of protection over my life and my children and family. If I had 10,000 tongues I couldn't thank you enough. There are so many people to thank and I can't name you all but I will say if you know you have been a part of my life and have experienced this journey with me, I want to say thank you.

To my dedication team of Xulon Press Company; Thank you so much for staying on top of me and supporting me for getting my testimony out. Thank you for being available when needed. My design crew at Xulon Press that did such an awesome job on my book cover THANK YOU! Sister Cheryl Pickett for being here for me and being available for my children and I. Thank you for being there to talk to and giving such great Godly and encouraging advice; not to mention when you get that mic in your hand in the choir stand. Melody Moore, my sister in Christ; girl, you are the best. I'm so glad God has placed you in my life when He did and how He did. Thank you for encouraging me. Such an anointed woman of God, I love you much.

My friends that have been telling me I should write a book and believing that I had a testimony to tell; LaToya Peoples, Nakisia McDanial, and Kenisha Stell. Terrance Green for being the best mentor for my children as well as myself. When I didn't think I could go on, you inspired me to move. Thanks for the encouraging word, the motivation you give the boys, and your prayers. and being the awesome man of God that you are. God was on time when He sent you. Thank you.

Last, but not least; my children for being my support, my backbone, and loving me for whom I am. I wouldn't be where I am if it wasn't for my four Blessings that God gave me to take care of. Daysheanah, Quincy, Da'Marea, and Xavier and my Granddaughter Zari (My Nu Nu); I love y'all with all in me. There are so many more people I have been blessed with in my life. The good and the bad. God Bless you all.